STANDARD SCHNAUZER

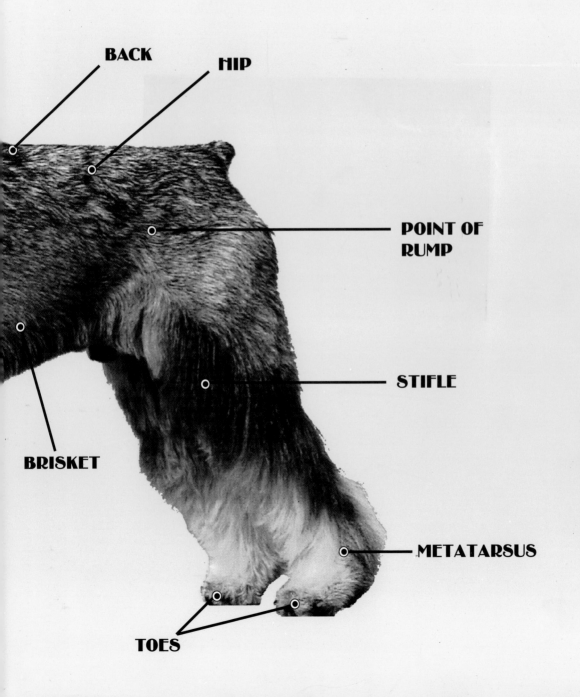

BACK

HIP

POINT OF
RUMP

STIFLE

BRISKET

METATARSUS

TOES

Title Page: AmCan. Ch. Oakwood Phantom Phlyer, UD owned by Barbara Dille.

Photographers: John Ashbey, Rich Bergman, Callea Photo, Cook Photography, C. Crumb, J. Day, Barbara Dille, Earl Graham Studios, Enid Evans, Isabelle Francais, Ed Hall, Judy Iby, Connie Reidner, Rich Schofield, Augie Smith, Susan Woog-Wagner, Lori Walker, Wiggins Photo, Yerusalimski Photo.

© by T.F.H. Publications, Inc.

Distributed in the UNITED STATES to the Pet Trade by T.F.H. Publications, Inc., One T.F.H. Plaza, Neptune City, NJ 07753; distributed in the UNITED STATES to the Bookstore and Library Trade by National Book Network, Inc. 4720 Boston Way, Lanham MD 20706; in CANADA to the Pet Trade by H & L Pet Supplies Inc., 27 Kingston Crescent, Kitchener, Ontario N2B 2T6; Rolf C. Hagen Inc., 3225 Sartelon St. Laurent-Montreal Quebec H4R 1E8; in CANADA to the Book Trade by Vanwell Publishing Ltd., 1 Northrup Crescent, St. Catharines, Ontario L2M 6P5 ; in ENGLAND by T.F.H. Publications, PO Box 15, Waterlooville PO7 6BQ; in AUSTRALIA AND THE SOUTH PACIFIC by T.F.H. (Australia), Pty. Ltd., Box 149, Brookvale 2100 N.S.W., Australia; in NEW ZEALAND by Brooklands Aquarium Ltd. 5 McGiven Drive, New Plymouth, RD1 New Zealand; in Japan by T.F.H. Publications, Japan—Jiro Tsuda, 10-12-3 Ohjidai, Sakura, Chiba 285, Japan; in SOUTH AFRICA by Lopis (Pty) Ltd., P.O. Box 39127, Booysens, 2016, Johannesburg, South Africa. Published by T.F.H. Publications, Inc.

MANUFACTURED IN THE
UNITED STATES OF AMERICA
BY T.F.H. PUBLICATIONS, INC.

STANDARD SCHNAUZER

1 66 6291

A COMPLETE AND RELIABLE HANDBOOK

Barbara M. Dille

RX-106

CONTENTS

DESCRIPTION OF THE STANDARD SCHNAUZER

The first impression of the Standard Schnauzer is that of a squarely built, energetic, medium-sized dog with a stiff wiry coat. He is robust and sturdy enough to be a working dog yet small enough in stature so as not to be overwhelming. These traits, combined with a coat that has minimal shedding and "doggy" odor, would lead some people to think that this is the ideal dog for everyone. However, it is what is found on the inside of this extremely agile body that has intrigued fanciers for centuries. This sometimes mischievous, quick and active dog is in reality a sensible, honest and reliable working dog with a superbly intelligent mind. This is the dog that is often called by fanciers "the dog with the human brain." The mind of the Standard Schnauzer does not develop well in kennel

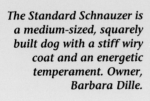

The Standard Schnauzer is a medium-sized, squarely built dog with a stiff wiry coat and an energetic temperament. Owner, Barbara Dille.

Holly Holst and her friend Ch. Tree Penelope, CD have participated in and excelled at the 4-H Canine project, which includes obedience and showmanship competitions.

situations, however. He thrives best on close interaction with his human family. Standard Schnauzers need the proper outlets for their above-average intelligence that only living as a family dog can provide. This breed has a very clever, inquisitive, creative and sometimes stubbornly determined mind, combined with a great sense of self-dignity. The Standard Schnauzer, although sometimes favoring one person, readily accepts all members of his human family as part of his inner circle. When raised properly, the Standard Schnauzer makes an affectionate friend and confidant for children. To his personal family, he is extremely loyal, playful and can have an interesting sense of humor. The family home is his castle and the arrival of each new stranger is announced with a deep bark that belies his mid-size stature. Only "real family" and a few select friends are privileged to the enthusiastic "wiggling from the inside out" welcome that Standard Schnauzers give their owners upon their arrival home. This very special and selective greeting has led fanciers of this breed worldwide to say: "Once owned by a Standard Schnauzer, any other breed is pale by comparison." This is a breed that excels as a home guardian, and with his intense vigor, inspires respect from all.

SIZE

The Standard Schnauzer is one of only a few truly mid-size dog breeds. Females should measure from 17 to 19 inches at the withers (top of shoulder) and the males should measure from 18 to 20 inches. The dogs range in weight from a low of approximately 35 pounds to a high of 48 pounds. This variation depends

All Standard Schnauzers are born black, but at around one week of age the salt and pepper colored dogs start to develop lighter markings. Owner, Lori Walker

on the sex, height and thickness of bone structure of the individual dog. A Standard Schnauzer is a dog that is strong enough and large enough to give his owner complete protection if needed yet still is small enough to be the perfect couch companion.

COAT COLORS

The double coat of the Standard Schnauzer is one of his most distinguished features. The outer coat consists of very coarse, harsh, stiff hairs that when seen against the grain, stand slightly up off the back, lying neither smooth nor flat. Undercoat is dense and consists of soft downy-like hairs. Both coats serve a different and definite purpose. The undercoat works

Black and salt and pepper are the only two acceptable coat colors in the Standard Schnauzer.

like insulation, keeping the dog warm in winter and cool in summer. The outer wire-coat offers excellent protection against the elements of nature and readily sheds dirt.

In the Standard Schnauzers described as "pepper and salt" color, the outer wire coat consists of a combination of black, white, and banded hairs. Each banded hair (depending on its age in the hair shaft) is a black hair with a white band or a white hair with a black band. This unique banding is what gives the coat its distinctive speckled appearance of having been sprinkled with "pepper and salt." On the body, length of the coat of a show dog ranges from ³/₄ of an inch to 2 inches in length. The coat lengthens over the eyes and muzzle to form eyebrows and a beard, thus giving the breed its distinctive appearance. The hair on the leg (furnishings) is longer than on the body and should be almost as harsh as the body coat. Coloration on the pepper and salt Standard Schnauzer fades out to a lighter gray in the eyebrows, beard and furnishings with a darker facial mustache-like mask overlaying the beard.

Solid black is the only other color that is permissible in the breed and it must have a solid black undercoat. Texture of the outer coat should have the same wiry feel in both colors.

EARS AND TAILS

In past years in the United States, most breeders have not paid much attention to the set or placement of the ear or to the thickness of the ear leather, nor have they paid much attention to the thickness or placement of the tail. This is because most Standard Schnauzers in the US are shown with cropped ears and docked tails. Recently there has been renewed interest in the uncropped ear in the United States. This increased interest is most likely because some countries in Europe have totally banned the showing of dogs with cropped ears. Sweden has even banned the docking of the tails. In the US, the tail of this breed is usually docked within the first three days of birth. It should be docked to a length that will be no longer than two inches nor shorter than one inch when the dog becomes an adult. Dewclaws are removed when the tail is docked.

SPECIAL ABILITIES

Although not as well known for their scenting ability as the Bloodhound, the Standard Schnauzer's attention to details and strong determined mind has made the sport of tracking a favorite of many Standard Schnauzer owners. Several owners have gone on to achieve the American Kennel Club title of Tracking Dog Excellent with their Standard Schnauzers.

Int. Ch. Argenta's Galathea hails from Sweden, where ear cropping has been banned. Owner, Argenta Kennels.

DESCRIPTION

Standard Schnauzers are intelligent dogs whose acute senses make them excellent Hearing Ear Dogs. Diane Aquillo and her Hearing Ear Dog "Hank."

Standards have been very successfully trained and used as Search and Rescue (SAR) dogs that find victims of natural and man-made disasters such as earthquakes and airplane crashes. SAR dogs are taught to air-scent for humans as opposed to ground-scent like the tracking dog. The dogs are taught to ride in a small boat (they can detect a human under water), to ride in a helicopter and to ride quietly with other dogs loose in a van. Jane Mayo owns Ch. Barnaba Von Krumchen, better known as "Bingo," who is a certified SAR dog with the paraprofessional search dog team DOGS-EAST. According to Jane, the Standard Schnauzer's inherent traits of endurance, independence and agility are perfect for the job of a SAR dog. His size is an asset for getting into small places and being lifted up onto a ledge or the next floor of a demolished building.

Organizations, such as the National Education for Assistance Dog Services (N.E.A.D.S.), have found that the Standard Schnauzer's size and extremely acute sense of hearing make them excellent candidates for use as Hearing Ear dogs. A Hearing Ear dog enables the deaf person to live a normal lifestyle in their soundless world. The Hearing Ear dog is taught to identify and alert their owner to a variety of auditory sounds.

The "assistance" or "service dog" is trained to be the arms and legs for a person in a wheelchair. In this endeavor, size does limit the Standard Schnauzer from being able to be used extensively as a full-service dog. However, PAWS FOR A CAUSE in Michigan and Canine Companions for Independence in California have successfully used them as assistance dogs for physically challenged people. These assistance dogs allow their owners to live more independent lives. Many more dogs of this amazing breed have been used successfully as certified Therapy Dogs that visit patients in nursing homes, hospitals and schools.

Currently, one Standard Schnauzer is being used in a very exciting and forward-thinking experiment in cancer detection research. This dog has been written up in medical journals and has been shown on television several times. "George," formally known as Ch. OTCh. Tailgates George Vonpickle, UDX is owned by retired police Sergeant Duane Pickel. Together they

Ch. Barnaba Von Krumchen, better known as "Bingo," is the first Standard Schnauzer to be certified as a Search and Rescue Dog. Owner, Jane Mayo.

have done some very remarkable work in helping doctors detect skin cancer in humans. "George" is a certified Physicians Assisting Canine (PAC) and according to his owner/trainer, he has been 100% accurate in finding skin cancer in the test trials. This shows again the extremely acute sense of smell with which this breed is blessed. Before his work in the medical field, "George" was a fully trained full time K-9 Police Dog working with Sergeant Pickel in the Tallahassee Police Bomb Squad Department.

Standards have been seen hiking with their masters, complete with their own backpack in wilderness areas. More than one owner has even used their Standard, instead of one of the more popular sporting breeds, to flush birds while hunting. The Standard Schnauzer has shown a strong herding instinct and several Standard Schnauzers have successfully passed herding dog instinct tests.

Versatility and adaptability are accurate descriptive words for Standard Schnauzers. Their performance capabilities are only limited by the imagination, interests, perseverance and ability of their master to direct their brilliant mind.

Opposite: Ch.Otch. Tailgate's George Vonpickel, UDX, shown with his handler Sergeant Duane Pickel, was a fully trained police dog and after retiring, became a Physicians Assistance Canine.

The trainability and versatility of the Standard Schnauzer allow them to be of great help to people with disabilities. Margaret "Muffi" Lavigne and her assistance dog "Rudi."

HISTORY OF THE STANDARD SCHNAUZER

No written record concerning how this breed was created has ever been found. However, we do know that as far back as the 14th century the Standard Schnauzer as we know it today appeared in several paintings by Albrecht Durer (1471—1528), most notably of which was in his *Madonna With the Many*

A depiction of a trio of early Schnauzers on a postcard from the German American Novelty Art series printed in Germany in early 1900.

Animals, painted in 1492. Later works of Durer contained seemingly the same dog as it aged. A tapestry, *The Crown of Thorns* by Lucas Cranach the Elder (1472-1553) dated 1501, along with other works of his, contained the likeness of a Standard Schnauzer. Rembrandt also painted some Standard Schnauzers, and one appears in an 18th century work of the English painter Sir Joshua Reynolds (1723-1792).

Many theories as to the origin of the breed have been discussed. The one most frequently heard theory

Although many people think the Standard Schnauzer is just a smaller version of his cousin the Giant Schnauzer, shown here, the Standard is actually the original type of all three breeds of Schnauzer.

is the theory that is probably the closest to the truth. This one relates to the 14th century tradesmen and farmers who traveled the countryside and to markets with carts laden with wares and produce. To protect these carts, the tradesmen needed, and bred in Germany, a guard dog of medium size that would not take up much space on the wagon yet would be strong enough to do the protection job required. Because they were excellent ratters, these dogs also did double duty back at home by keeping the stable and the house rat free. The breeders involved in creating this dog most likely crossed the black German Poodle and the gray Wolfspitz with Wire-Haired Pinscher stock.

The Standard Schnauzer is the origin of the three breeds of Schnauzers. Many people are under the misconception that the Standard Schnauzer is just a larger or smaller version of his more popular cousins, the Miniature Schnauzer and Giant Schnauzer. Truth of the matter is that other breeds of dogs were introduced into the bloodlines of the Standard Schnauzer to develop the smaller and larger versions. With the introduction of the new bloodlines to develop the Miniature and the Giant Schnauzers, the results, although bearing a strong physical resemblance to the original, produced two new breeds. The family name that the three distinct breeds share was probably derived in the early years from their appearance. With the German word for muzzle being

"Schnauze," the breed with a beard on the muzzle became the Schnauzer. In Germany where the breed originated, the three Schnauzers were put in the same club as the Pinchers where they remain today.

At the Third German International Show in Hanover in 1879, Wire-haired Pinschers, as they were referred to then, were exhibited for the first time on record. Three dogs, owned by C. Burger, were entered from the Wurttemberg Kennel. The first prize winner was named "Schnauzer;" "Betti" and "Anni" won second prizes. From that time on, all dogs of that breed were called Schnauzers.

The Standard Schnauzer was used during WWI by the Red Cross for guard duty and the German Army used them as dispatch carriers. Their dependability, a strong breed characteristic, made them favorites of both groups. Records show that the first importation of the breed into the United States was around the year 1900. However, it was not until after WWI that the Standard Schnauzer was brought to the United States in any significant numbers. Once American dog fanciers and breeders were introduced to the Standard Schnauzer, the breed quickly gained popularity. In 1925, The Schnauzer Club of America was formed, and included fanciers of both the Standard and Miniature Schnauzer breeds. In 1933 the club was forced to divide. This division enabled the two sizes to continue to be registered as separate breeds with the American Kennel Club. The name of the original club was changed to the Standard Schnauzer Club of America (S.S.C.A.) with William D. Goff as the first President. Since then, several local specialty clubs devoted to the breed have formed around the country under the auspices of this parent club.

The modern Standard Schnauzer is groomed and conditioned to look like the exceptional purebred dog he is.

The Standard Schnauzer has never experienced the same popularity with the public as their Miniature and Giant cousins. Nevertheless, according to American Kennel Club registration, steady growth was seen for a number of years thanks to a small group of enthusiastic fanciers. In 1952, records show that 280 puppies were registered. By 1962 the number registered in that year rose to 308 puppies. The year 1976 saw the peak in popularity with a total of 785 Standard Schnauzer puppies registered. Since the seventies, the popularity of the breed has slowly declined. In the year 1996, the breed dropped to a low of only a total

This postcard, dated 1908, shows the rust-yellow colored Schnauzer that was described in the German standard published in 1880.

of 551 puppies registered with the AKC, and the breed ranking for the year slid down to #100. This current lack of popularity of the Standard Schnauzer has made the task of finding a puppy not always an easy one. Prospective owners often have to travel across two or more state lines to find a puppy or young adult, especially if the sex of the animal is an important issue. The best place to get a good quality Standard Schnauzer puppy is through a breeder that belongs to the Standard Schnauzer Club of America or one of the regional local specialty Standard Schnauzer clubs. Names and addresses of the current secretaries of these clubs can be obtained from the American Kennel Club.

SHOWING YOUR STANDARD SCHNAUZER

So versatile is the Standard Schnauzer that even his classification for show purposes has been subject to debate. When first imported into the United States, the Standard Schnauzer was placed in the Working Group. It was during the 1920s that the breed, along with its cousin the Miniature Schnauzer, was moved into the Terrier Group. By 1945, the breed was moved back into the Working Group with its larger cousin, the Giant Schnauzer, where it has remained until this day.

Ch. Oakwood Phantom Phlyer is a perfect example of the adaptability and versatility of the Standard Schnauzer, as he often competed in both conformation and obedience rings at the same show. Owner, Barbara Dille.

Ch. Geistvoll On The Move is a fine example of the robust, heavy-set dog as stated in the standard. Owners, Jim and Renee Pope.

Just to add further confusion, in Germany the breed is in the Working Group, while in England The Kennel Club places the breed in the Non-Sporting Group. Standard Schnauzer breeders, judges and show handlers in the United States frequently discuss the question of which AKC group of dogs best suits the breed. The Standard Schnauzer is currently classified with the AKC as part of the Working Group and this is a designation that is strongly supported by the Standard Schnauzer Club of America.

The one thing that the judge is looking for in the Standard Schnauzer in the show ring is the conformation or structure of the dog. In past years, outstanding representatives of this breed have been shown in the conformation ring that have come close to fitting the visual picture of the S.S.C.A. written standard for the breed. Many outstanding dogs, past and present, have won multiple Group and Best in Show awards handled exclusively by their owners who take great pride in showing their special pet. The showing of these dogs is normally limited to the regional area of the country where the owner or handler resides.

In 1993, Parsifal di Casa Netzer, an Italian bred dog, was sent to the United States by his breeder

Gabrio del Torre to obtain his American Championship. "Pa," as he is known to his friends in the kennel, continued to be extensively shown throughout the country by a professional through 1996. This Standard Schnauzer, by defeating more show dogs than any other dog in 1996, won the honor of being crowned the number one show dog for the year. Frosting was put on his cake in February 1997 by his handler winning the prestigious Westminster Kennel Club dog show. Truly a hard record for any breed to surpass, let alone another Standard Schnauzer in the years to come.

OFFICIAL STANDARD FOR THE STANDARD SCHNAUZER

Over the past century in this country, the official standard that breeders and judges in the conformation dog world have used as a guideline when breeding and judging the Satndard Schnuazer has seen a few subtle changes. Likewise, the official standard used in the US differs slightly from the official standard used in Germany. Grooming techniques used today in the US are much more involved than those used in the beginning of the century and are very different than the way the breed is presently shown in European countries. In Europe, the two acceptable coat colors of salt and pepper and black are not allowed to be interbred. In the United States, salt and peppers are quite often found in the pedigrees of the black Standards. Remaining constant over the years and throughout the world is the perfect mid-sized, energetic, alert, "always ready to do something" attitude of the wonderful companion and guardian of the home known as the Standard Schnauzer.

The following is the American Kennel Club Standard for the Standard Schnauzer.

General Appearance—The Standard Schnauzer is a robust, heavy-set dog, sturdily built with good muscle and plenty of bone; square-built in proportion of body length to height. His rugged build and dense harsh coat are accentuated by the hallmark of the breed, the arched eyebrows and the bristly mustache and whiskers. *Faults*—Any deviation that detracts from the Standard Schnauzer's desired general appearance of a robust, active, square-built wire-coated dog. Any deviation from the specifications in the Standard is to be considered a fault and should be penalized in proportion to the extent of the deviation.

Opposite: Not only a professionally handled show dog, Ch. Vortac Vindicator, CD is also a certified Canine Good Citizen and Therapy Dog—the beloved companion of Cathy Burdick.

Size, Proportion, Substance—Ideal height at the highest point of the shoulder blades, 18 ¹/₂ to 19 ¹/₂ inches for males and 17 ¹/₂ to 18 ¹/₂ inches for females. Dogs measuring over or under these limits must be faulted in proportion to the extent of the deviation. Dogs measuring more than one-half inch over or under these limits must be disqualified. The height at the highest point of the withers equals the length from breastbone to point of the rump.

Head—Head strong, rectangular, and elongated; narrowing slightly from the ears to the eyes and again to the tip of the nose. The total length of the head is about one half the length of the back measured from the withers to the set-on of the tail. The head matches the sex and substance of the dog. *Expression* alert, highly intelligent, spirited. *Eyes* medium size; dark brown; oval in shape and turned forward; neither round nor protruding. The brow is arched and wiry, but vision is not impaired nor eyes hidden by too long an eyebrow.

Ears set high, evenly shaped with moderate thickness of leather and carried erect when cropped. If

Ch. Cimarron Ensign Cody Skico owned by Lori Walker shows the correct cropped ears.

The Standard Schnauzer's ears should be high set and evenly shaped with moderate thickness of leather. This handsome dog shows off his natural ears.

uncropped, they are of medium size, V-shaped and mobile so that they break at skull level and are carried forward with the inner edge close to the cheek. **Faults**—Prick, or hound ears.

Skull *(Occiput to Stop)* moderately broad between the ears with the width of the skull not exceeding two thirds the length of the skull. The skull must be flat; neither domed nor bumpy; skin unwrinkled. There is a slight stop which is accentuated by the wiry brows. **Muzzle** strong, and both parallel and equal in length to the top skull; it ends in a moderately blunt wedge with wiry whiskers accenting the rectangular shape of the head. The topline of the muzzle is parallel with the topline of the skull. **Nose** is large, black and full. The lips should be black, tight and not overlapping. **Cheeks**—Well developed chewing muscles, but not so much that "cheekiness" disturbs the rectangular head form.

Bite—A full complement of white teeth, with a strong, sound scissors bite. The canine teeth are strong and well developed with the upper incisors slightly overlapping and engaging the lower. The upper and lower jaws are powerful and neither over-shot nor undershot. *Faults*—A level bite is considered undesirable but a lesser fault than an overshot or undershot mouth.

Neck, Topline, Body—*Neck* strong, of moderate thickness and length, elegantly arched and blending cleanly into the shoulders. The skin is tight, fitting closely to the dry throat with no wrinkles or dewlaps. The *topline* of the back should not be absolutely horizontal, but should have a descending slope from the first vertebra of the withers to the faintly curved croup and set-on of the tail. Back strong, firm, straight and short. Loin well developed, with the distance from the last rib to the hips as short as possible.

Body compact, strong, short-coupled and sub-stantial so as to permit great flexibility and agility. *Faults*—Too slender or shelly; too bulky or coarse.

Chest of medium width with well sprung ribs, and if it could be seen in cross section would be oval. The breastbone is plainly discernible. The brisket must descend at least to the elbows and ascend gradually to the rear with the belly moderately drawn up. *Fault*—Excessive tuck-up. *Croup* full and slightly rounded. *Tail* set moderately high and carried erect. It is docked to not less that one inch nor more than two inches. *Fault*—Squirrel tail.

Forequarters—*Shoulders*—The sloping shoulder blades are strongly muscled, yet flat and well laid back so that the rounded upper ends are in a nearly vertical line above the elbows. They slope well forward to the point where they join the upper arm, forming as nearly as possible a right angle when seen from the side. Such an angulation permits the maximum forward extension of the forelegs without binding or effort. *Forelegs* straight, vertical, and without any curvature when seen from all sides; set moderately far apart, with heavy bone; elbows set close to the body and pointing directly to the rear. Dewclaws on the forelegs may be removed.

Feet small and compact, round with thick pads and strong black nails. The toes are well closed and arched (cat's paws) and pointing straight ahead.

Hindquarters—Strongly muscled, in balance with the forequarters, never appearing higher than the shoulders. Thighs broad with well bent stifles. The second thigh, from knee to hock is approximately parallel with an extension of the upper neck line. The legs, from the clearly defined hock joint to the feet, are short and perpendicular to the ground and, when viewed from the rear, are parallel to each other. Dewclaws, if any, on the hind legs are generally removed. Feet as in front.

Coat—Tight, hard, wiry and as thick as possible, composed of a soft, close undercoat and a harsh outer coat which, when seen against the grain, stands up off the back, lying neither smooth nor flat. The outer coat (body coat) is trimmed (by plucking) only to accent the body outline. As coat texture is of the greatest importance, a dog may be considered in a show coat with back hair measuring from ³/₄ to 2 inches in length. Coat on the ears, head, neck, chest, belly and under the tail may be closely trimmed to give

The Standard Schnauzer is a robust, sturdily built dog with good muscle and a rugged harsh coat. AmCan. Ch. Chateau Palos Pinot Noir, CDX owned by Donald and Mary Lou Just.

In salt-and-pepper-colored Standard Schnauzers, the color may fade to a light gray or silver white in the eyebrows, whiskers, chest and legs.

the desired typical appearance of the breed. On the muzzle and over the eyes the coat lengthens to form the beard and eyebrows; the hair on the legs is longer than that on the body. These "furnishings" should be of harsh texture and should not be so profuse as to detract from the neat appearance or working capabilities of the dog. *Faults*—Soft, smooth, curly, wavy or shaggy; too long or too short; too sparse or lacking undercoat; excessive furnishing; lack of furnishings.

Color—Pepper and salt or pure black. *Pepper and Salt*—The typical pepper and salt color of the topcoat results from the combination of black and white hairs, and white hairs banded with black. Acceptable are all shades of pepper and salt and dark iron gray to silver gray. Ideally, pepper and salt Standard Schnauzers have a gray undercoat, but a tan or fawn undercoat is not to be penalized. It is desirable to have a darker facial mask that harmonizes with the particular shade of coat color. Also, in pepper and salt dogs, the pepper and salt mixture may fade out to light gray or silver white in the eyebrows, whiskers, cheeks, under throat, across chest, under tail, leg furnishings, under body,

Professionally handled AmCan. Ch. Von Schatten's Shayna Maidel, owned by Leona Mintz, shows the proper color and texture of the black Standard Schnauzer.

and inside legs. **Black**—Ideally the black Standard Schnauzer should be a true rich color, free from any fading or discoloration or any mixture of gray or tan hairs. The undercoat should also be solid black. However, increased age or continued exposure to the sun may cause a certain amount of fading and burning. A small white smudge on the chest is not a fault. Loss of color as a result of scars from cuts and bites is not a fault. **Faults**—Any colors other than specified,

OF
ED
VALLEY
CLUB
ASHBEY

and any shadings or mixtures thereof in the topcoat such as rust, brown, red, yellow or tan; absence of peppering; spotting or striping; a black streak down the back; or a black saddle without typical salt and pepper coloring—and gray hairs in the coat of a black; in blacks, any undercoat color other than black.

Gait—Sound, strong, quick, free, true and level gait with powerful, well-angulated hindquarters that reach out and cover ground. The forelegs reach out in a stride balancing that of the hindquarters. At a trot, the back remains firm and level, without swaying, rolling or reaching. When viewed from the rear, the feet, though they may appear to travel close when trotting, must not cross or strike. Increased speed causes feet to converge toward the center line of gravity. **Faults**—Crabbing or weaving; padding; rolling; swaying; short; choppy; stiff; stilted rear action; front legs that throw out or in (East and West movers); hackney gait; crossing over; or striking in front or rear.

Ch. Pepper Tree Bel Air Ryan owned by Marie Adickes and Arden Holst.

The Standard Schnauzer thrives in a family environment and loves to be around people. The author and her grandson get a big kiss from their Schnauzer friend.

Temperament—The Standard Schnauzer has highly developed senses, intelligence, aptitude for training, fearlessness, endurance and resistance against weather and illness. His nature combines high-spirited temperament with extreme reliability.

Faults—In weighing the seriousness of a fault, greatest consideration should be given to deviation from the desired alert, highly intelligent, spirited, reliable character of the Standard Schnauzer. Dogs that are shy or appear to be highly nervous should be seriously faulted and dismissed from the ring. Vicious dogs shall be disqualified.

Disqualifications—Males under 18 inches or over 20 inches in height. Females under 17 inches or over 19 inches in height. Vicious dogs.
Approved February 9, 1991
Effective March 27, 1991

GROOMING THE STANDARD SCHNAUZER

The owner of the Standard Schnauzer kept strictly as a companion and family pet has two options as to how the coat can be maintained.

The first and easiest option is to take the dog to your local groomer and have them machine clip the body coat. Clipping, requiring a trip to the groomer approximately every six to eight weeks, is faster and easier on the dog and the pocketbook. Many breeders routinely clip their old timers that are no longer being used for breeding or showing. However, clipping does make

If you want to show your Standard Schnauzer, he must have his coat hand plucked, as the texture of the coat is a major consideration in the show ring.

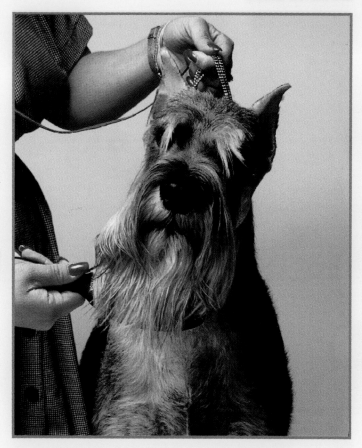

Regular washing and combing of your Schnauzer's beard is very important to keep the hair clean and prevent mats from forming.

the coat much softer every time it is done. The characteristic pepper and salt coloration gradually fades out and turns to a solid gray, and the black dogs start to lose the shine to their coat.

The second option is to hand-strip the body coat. To use this option you must either learn how to hand-strip (pluck) the hard wire topcoat yourself or find an experienced handler or breeder that is willing to do it. Hand-stripping requires a minimum of twice a week maintenance in a dog being actively shown or approximately two or three times a year, depending on the texture and harshness of the coat, for the well-maintained pet.

Hand stripping or plucking of the jacket is the removal of the dead hair from the hair shaft. The hair is not cut. This method keeps the hard, wire texture of the body coat that is one of the outstanding characteristics of this wonderful breed. The dog must be maintained in this fashion if the dog is being shown in the breed ring, as the texture of the coat is a major consideration in the show dog.

A word of warning: Be very careful when you first talk to a local all-breed groomer about working on your Standard Schnauzer. Be specific and request that the dog be "hand- stripped" or "plucked" if that is the method you have decided you want to use. If you do not specifically use this terminology, you could return later to find that your dog has been machine stripped (clipped) of all his hair, including that on the muzzle and legs.

The part of the coat that forms the eyebrows, mustache, beard and furnishings does not shed like the jacket. These areas, regardless of whether the

If you take your Schnauzer to a professional groomer, make sure he is familiar with the proper areas to use scissors when working with a Schnauzer's coat.

body coat is machine clipped or hand-stripped, should be carefully trimmed with thinning shears and scissors to neaten up and maintain the characteristic crisp outline.

Whichever method is used to maintain the dog's coat, a daily washing of the beard is required to prevent a build-up of food particles. Daily combing of the beard and furnishings will prevent mats from forming. A brushing of the body coat with a stiff bristle brush twice a week will keep the skin and body coat in excellent condition and odor and dirt free. Bathing the Standard Schnauzer is not necessary unless they decide to revert to their wild canine instincts of rolling in some horrible smelly mess they found in the garden.

TEETH

Though Standard Schnauzers are blessed with strong teeth and gums, many dogs will develop plaque on their teeth as they grow older. By brushing the teeth weekly, and making sure the dog has lots of Nylabones® to play with, trips to the veterinarian for a major tooth cleaning job can be reduced. Introduce your puppy at a very young age to a weekly tooth brushing as a routine part of grooming. This brushing can be done with either a soft baby toothbrush or several layers of gauze wrapped around your finger. The brush or gauze should be moistened slightly with plain water and then lightly scrub each tooth on the top and bottom jaws to remove the plaque.

Brush your puppy's teeth weekly and provide him with plenty of Nylabones® to promote productive chewing.

OWNING A STANDARD SCHNAUZER

Standard Schnauzer's are above average when compared with most other breeds of dogs concerning health. They live an average of 13 to 16 extremely active years. Most Standard Schnauzer owners find that only an annual visit to their veterinarian for a check-up and routine shots are required.

Occasionally, problems that occur in other breeds will crop up in the Standard Schnauzer. Some of these problems pose severe health problems to the dogs and big heartaches to their breeders and owners. The Standard Schnauzer Club of America recently formed a new health committee to try to insure that no disease or problem that is possibly genetic in nature ever becomes a widespread problem in this otherwise very healthy breed. It was only through the efforts of concerned breeders of Standard Schnauzers many years ago that the problem of hip dysplasia has been sharply reduced in our breed in the United States. The Standard Schnauzer Club of America (S.S.C.A.) presently continues to recommend that all

The Standard Schnauzer is a very adaptable dog that will get along with other pets if introduced to them at an early age. Truwick's Hard Copy and Plane owned by Enid Evans.

The Standard Schnauzer needs daily exercise at a brisk steady pace to keep in prime physical condition.

breeding stock owned by members be radiographed free of hip dysplasia. Although eye problems rarely show up in the Standard Schnauzer, the S.S.C.A. also recommends that breeding stock be tested annually.

The majority of Standard Schnauzer breeders are working together to keep the breed as free of genetic problems as possible. We currently enjoy saying, and wish to continue to be able to say, that the major problem leading to cause of death in this breed is just plain old age.

BREED REQUIREMENTS

The Standard Schnauzer is a very adaptable dog. Although some breeders will not sell a puppy to anyone that does not have a fenced yard and others will require at least one non-working family member, the truth is that the Standard fits into almost any lifestyle or enviroment. Often the Standard will accept sharing the house with cats, especially if he is introduced to them at a young age. However, small members of the rodent family kept as pets should be always kept in secure cages to ensure their safety. In many Standard Schnauzers today, the hereditary instincts of their origins as rat-catchers can be extremely strong.

The Standard Schnauzer does need ample exercise, not only for the body but also for the mind. The adult dog should at the minimum get the equivalent of a brisk one-mile walk at least three times a day. To keep the dog in prime physical condition, these walks should be brisk enough to keep the dog at a steady trotting pace. As a puppy he is constantly exploring, learning and testing his limits. As adults they are always ready for a walk in the woods, a ride in the car, a training session or any other activity that allows them to be with their owners. They are dog that know how to be on the alert, even when snoozing by their owners' feet.

This European show dog is Mekaterina-Concorde from Russia owned by E. Yerusalimsky.

THE QUESTION OF SPAYING/NEUTERING

If a female puppy was purchased as a pet for the family, spaying her at approximately six months of age is best. By spaying the Standard Schnauzer before her first estrus cycle (heat cycle), the risk of a possible unwanted litter of mixed breed puppies is eliminated. Spaying at this young age has less of a risk factor to the female and is usually less expensive. Spaying may prevent metritis and pyometra, both common in adult intact females, or other serious health problems that affect the unaltered female dog.

Castration or neutering of the male dog has even more significant results. Neutering the male can be done anytime, but for best results it should be done before one year of age. Many undesirable behavior problems, such as urine marking, mounting and aggression toward other animals, can be lessened or eliminated entirely, depending on the age at which the surgery is done.

Spaying or neutering does not cause a dog to get fat. Lack of exercise and overindulgence by the owner is the primary cause of obesity in the Standard Schnauzer.

If you plan to show your newly acquired Standard Schnauzer in the conformation ring, you cannot spay or neuter your dog. The conformation show ring is a competition designed to show off the best breeding stock available. However, a surgically altered Champion can be shown in the Veteran class when they are old enough, providing there is no Group or Best in Show competition offered at the show. Both sexes, even when spayed or neutered, are eligible to compete in any competitive performance event, such as obedience, agility, or herding.

Responsible breeders will be concerned with maintaining the quality of the breed and will always strive to produce the best puppies possible.

YOUR PUPPY'S NEW HOME

Before bringing your new puppy home, ask the breeder of your puppy exactly what supplies, toys and food you will need to ensure a smooth transition for the puppy into his new home. If you are planning to buy products that will last the expected 12- to 15-year life span of the Standard Schnauzer, you will probably need a week or more before the arrival of the pup to shop around for the best prices and quality.

It is always better to collect the puppy as early in the day as possible. In most instances this will mean that the puppy has a few hours with your family before it is time to retire for his first night's sleep away from his former home.

If the breeder is local, then you may not need any form of box to place the puppy in when you bring him home. A member of the family can hold the pup in his lap—duly protected by some towels just in case the puppy becomes car sick! Be sure to advise the breeder at what time you hope to arrive for the puppy, as this will obviously influence the feeding of the pup that morning or afternoon. If you arrive early in the day, then they will likely only give the pup a light breakfast so as to reduce the risk of travel sickness.

If the trip will be of a few hours duration, you should take a travel crate with you. The crate will provide your pup with a safe place to lie down and rest during the trip. During the trip, the puppy will no doubt wish to relieve his bowels, so you will have to make a few stops. On a long journey you may need a rest yourself, and can take the opportunity to let the puppy get some fresh air. However, do not let the puppy walk where there may have been a lot of other dogs because he might pick up an infection. Also, if he relieves his bowels at such a time, do not just leave the feces where they were dropped. This is the height of irre-sponsibility. It has resulted in many public parks and other places actually banning dogs. You can purchase poop-scoops from your pet shop and should have them with you whenever you are taking the dog out where he might foul a public place.

Your journey home should be made as quickly as possible. If it is a hot day, be sure the car interior is amply supplied with fresh air. It should never be too hot or too cold for the puppy. The pup must never be placed where he might be subject to a draft. If the journey requires an overnight stop at a motel, be aware that other guests will not appreciate a puppy crying half the night. You must regard the puppy as a baby and comfort him so he does not cry for long

Your young Schnauzer may fit in your trousers, but a crate is the safest way to transport your puppy home from the breeders.

periods. The worst thing you can do is to shout at or smack him. This will mean your relationship is off to a really bad start. You wouldn't smack a baby, and your puppy is still very much just this.

If the breeder of your puppy lives such a great distance from you that picking up the puppy by automobile is impossible, you might be forced to have the pup shipped to you by commercial airline. This is not as traumatic an experience for the puppy as might be expected. Most Standard Schnauzer puppies that have a normal temperament survive this experience just fine. I do recommend taking your breeder's advice as to which airline they have had the best experiences with shipping other puppies. I advise shipping the pup, when possible, by the method the airlines call "counter to counter" rather than by air cargo. Normally, this is a less expensive method of shipping, and more importantly, this method will shorten the time that the pup is in transit by two or more hours.

ON ARRIVING HOME

Upon arrival home, offer your pup a drink of water and then take him to the area that you have designated to be his bathroom area. After the pup has had an opportunity to relieve himself, allow him to explore for

a few minutes the room where his crate will be kept. Resist the temptation to indulge in playing with the pup for an hour or so and allow the pup to rest in his crate quietly during this time. When the pup awakens from his nap, take him immediately to the designated bathroom area. Upon completion of his bathroom duties, you can offer the pup his first meal in his new home. Do not overfeed him at his first meal nor worry if he does not want to eat. Some pups take several days to adjust to the total change in their environment.

Although it is an obvious temptation, you should not invite friends and neighbors around to see the new arrival until he has had at least 48 hours in

Puppies are naturally inquisitive, and the kitchen can hold many dangers for a curious young pup. Closely supervise your puppy when at home. Owner, Lori Walker.

Candi and Allison are great friends, but make sure your child is taught the proper way to treat and handle dogs before leaving them alone together.

which to settle down. Indeed, if you can delay this longer then do so, especially if the puppy is not fully vaccinated. At the very least, the visitors might introduce some local bacteria on their clothing that the puppy is not immune to. This aspect is always a risk when a pup has been moved some distance, so the fewer people the pup meets in the first week or so the better.

DANGERS IN THE HOME

Your home holds many potential dangers for a little mischievous puppy, so you must think about these in advance and be sure he is protected from them. The more obvious are as follows:

Open Fires. All open fires should be protected by a mesh screen guard so there is no danger of the pup being burned by spitting pieces of coal or wood.

Electrical Wires. Puppies just love chewing on things, so be sure that all electrical appliances are neatly hidden from view and are not left plugged in when not in use. It is not sufficient simply to turn the plug switch to the off position—pull the plug from the socket.

Open Doors. A door would seem a pretty innocuous object, yet with a strong draft it could kill or injure a puppy easily if it is slammed shut. Always ensure there is no risk of this happening. It is most likely during warm weather when you have windows or outside doors open and a sudden gust of wind blows through.

Balconies. If you live in a high-rise building, obviously the pup must be protected from falling. Be sure he cannot get through any railings on your patio, balcony, or deck.

Ponds and Pools. A garden pond or a swimming pool is a very dangerous place for a little puppy to be near. Be sure it is well screened so there is no risk of the pup falling in. It takes barely a minute for a pup—or a child—to drown.

The Kitchen. While many puppies will be kept in the kitchen, at least while they are toddlers and not able to control their bowel movements, this is a room full of danger—especially while you are cooking. When cooking and eating, keep the puppy in his crate. This "time out" crating will not only protect him from harm but prevent the bad habit of begging at the table from forming.

Be aware, when using washing machines, that more than one puppy has clambered in and decided to have a nap and received a wash instead! If you leave the washing machine door open and leave the room for any reason, then be sure to check inside the machine before you close the door and switch on.

Small Children. Toddlers and small children should never be left unsupervised with puppies. In spite of such advice it is amazing just how many people not only do this but also allow children to pull and maul pups. They should be taught from the outset that a puppy is not a plaything to be dragged about the home.

Children who cannot respect the fact that this new pup is a virtually helpless baby animal should be denied the privilege of playing with the puppy without close supervision of an adult member of the family. Another factor to be aware of is that it is not at all unusual for the youngest child in the family to be jealous of all the attention the new pup is receiving. Sometimes the child will act up and show signs of sibling rivalry. If this is the case, show the child some extra attention and find a constructive way to help the child participate in the daily chores of raising the puppy.

Children must be shown how to lift a puppy so it is safe. Failure by you to correctly educate your children about dogs could one day result in their getting a very nasty bite or scratch. When a puppy is lifted, his weight must always be supported. To lift the pup, first place your right hand under his chest. Next, secure

The first few nights your puppy spends away from his dam and littermates may be lonely for him. Spend extra time with him and make him as comfortable as possible. This puppy's ears are taped to stay in the proper erect position. Owner, Kathy Koehler.

the pup by using your left hand to hold his neck. Now you can lift him and bring him close to your chest. Never lift a pup by his ears and, while he can be lifted by the scruff of his neck where the fur is loose, there is no reason ever to do this, so don't.

Beyond the dangers already cited you may be able to think of other ones that are specific to your home—steep basement steps or the like. Go around your home and check out all potential problems—you'll be glad you did.

THE FIRST NIGHT

The first few nights a puppy spends away from his mother and littermates are quite traumatic for him. He will feel very lonely, maybe cold, and will certainly miss the heartbeat of his siblings when sleeping. To help overcome his loneliness it may help to place a clock next to his bed—one with a loud tick. This will in some way soothe him, as the clock ticks to a rhythm not dissimilar from a heart beat. A cuddly toy may also help in the first few weeks. You might also place a radio near his crate tuned to a station of soft music or even an all-night talk station. The radio will help to drown out extraneous noises that might awaken the pup in the middle of the night.

If the pup does whimper in the night, there are two things you should not do. One is to get up and chastise him, because he will not understand why you are shouting at him; and the other is to rush to comfort him every time he cries because he will quickly realize that if he wants you to come running all he needs to do is to holler loud enough!

By all means give your puppy some extra attention on his first night, but after this quickly refrain from so doing. The pup will cry for a while but then settle down and go to sleep. Some pups are, of course, worse than others in this respect, so you must use balanced judgment in the matter.

OTHER PETS

If you have other pets in the home, the new puppy must be introduced to them under careful supervision. Some adult dogs do not know what to do with a puppy. It is not unusual for some adult dogs to be jealous and feel threatened by the new intruder. Other adult dogs can actually be afraid of this pup they view as a whirling dervish. If the adult dog wants to snap or otherwise harm the pup, keep the pup in the crate for a few days while the older dog is loose in the room. This will enable the older dog some time to get used to the smells and sounds of the new pup and sharing your attention.

Cats can usually take care of themselves and will generally jump clear of pups and watch them from a suitable vantage point. Eventually, they will meet at ground level. The cat will set the rules and let the puppy know its limits and the two soon will become friends. Other pet animals such as small rodents, rabbits and exotics are best kept safe and away from the predatory instincts of the Standard Schnauzer.

THE DOG CRATE

Some owners are reluctant to use a dog crate because they do not understand animal behavior and how a dog thinks. In the wild state, the dog is raised in a den and continues to use a natural den for its entire life for the purposes of sanctuary, sleeping and raising young. Humans have taken this natural denning instinct of the dog one step further. By incorporating in our homes an artificial manmade den hereafter called a crate, we are using these natural instincts to

Relaxing during a trip to the beach, the young Ch. Ahrenfelds Fortune Hunter has had a very busy day.

our advantage while we teach our puppy house manners.

The fact that some people view the crate as a very confining space is strictly a human viewpoint. No matter what your neighbors might say, you are not being cruel. The crate should never be used as a form of punishment. Instead it acts like the proverbial "ounce of prevention" as it enables you to prevent an unsupervised pup from having costly house-soiling or chewing accidents in your home.

Young puppies, like young toddlers, must have constant supervision during their waking hours. With a pup, praise or reprimand must be given within three seconds of doing something in order for the puppy to associate that particular act with your response.

Introduction to the crate should be done in an upbeat yet fact-of-life firm way. Place the pup in the crate and give him a very small treat or a favorite toy and immediately call the pup back out. Repeat this procedure five or six times. Then when the pup is in the crate, close the door for a minute or two and then let the pup out. Repeat this procedure two or three more times during the first day, gradually lengthening the time the crate door is closed. If the pup falls asleep outside the crate during this first day, quietly pick up the pup and place him in the crate to finish his nap. Once introduced properly to the crate, in a matter of days the puppy will find that the crate is a secure haven from the big and sometimes confusing outside world of humans.

Until he has learned proper house manners, the new puppy should be kept in his crate during the day and at night whenever adult supervision is not possible. Provide soft, washable bedding material, such as towels or a bathmat, in the crate along with his favorite Nylabone®. Do not place food or water inside the crate. Remove collar and tags from the pup when inside the crate to prevent possible entanglement.

HOUSETRAINING

Training the young Standard Schnauzer pup to use only its designated bathroom area outside for elimination purposes is not too difficult a feat if you use a crate properly to help in the process.

The prime times that a puppy will urinate and defecate are upon awakening from sleep, shortly after eating or drinking, and during or immediately following strenuous activity. The young puppy does not have a great holding capacity but thankfully this holding capacity does improve fairly quickly. For the first week you might find that you have to take the pup out every hour in order to keep your floors clean. Depending on the individual pup, this will gradually stretch into four-hour intervals and longer. Keep in mind that the pup will not be able to control his elimination functions fully during the day until he can keep his crate clean and dry for at least eight hours at night.

Whenever the pup is taken on a leash to the designated bathroom area, have every member of the family use a command like "Potty time" or "Business first." If you repeat this phrase before, during, and after the pup eliminates, you will be surprised at how quickly the pup will associate the command with the act of elimination. Shortly, your trips outside with the pup for elimination purposes will be very brief ones lasting only a minute or two each time. Remember to lavish praise within three seconds of the act of elimination in order for the pup to associate the command-act-praise sequence correctly.

THE EARLY DAYS

You will no doubt be given much advice on how to bring up your puppy. This will come from dog-owning friends, neighbors, and through articles and books you may read on the subject. Some of the advice will be sound, some will be nothing short of rubbish. What you should do above all else is to keep an open mind and let common sense prevail over prejudice and worn-out ideas that have been handed down over the centuries. There is no one way that is superior to all others, no more than there is no one dog that is exactly a replica of another. Each is an individual and must always be regarded as such.

A dog never becomes disobedient, unruly, or a menace to society without the full consent of his owner. Your puppy may have many limitations, but the singular biggest limitation he is confronted with in so many instances is his owner's inability to understand his needs and how to cope with them.

IDENTIFICATION

It is a sad reflection on our society that the number of dogs and cats stolen every year runs into many thousands. To these can be added the number that get lost. If you do not want your cherished pet to be lost or stolen, then you should see that he is carrying a permanent identification number, as well as a temporary tag on his collar.

Permanent markings come in the form of tattoos placed either inside the pup's ear flap, or on the inner side of a pup's upper rear leg. The number given is then recorded with one of the national registration companies. Research laboratories will not purchase dogs carrying numbers as they realize these are clearly someone's pet, and not abandoned animals. As a result, thieves will normally abandon dogs so marked and this at least gives the dog a chance to be taken to the police or the dog pound, when the number can be traced and the dog reunited with its family. The only problem with this method at this time is that there are a number of registration bodies, so it is not always apparent which one the dog is registered with (as you provide the actual number). However, each registration body is aware of his competitors and will normally be happy to supply their addresses. Those holding the dog can check out which one you are with. It is not a perfect system, but until such is developed it's the best available.

A temporary tag takes the form of a metal or plastic disk large enough for you to place the dog's name and your phone number on it—maybe even your address as well. In virtually all places you will be required to obtain a license for your puppy. This may not become applicable until the pup is six months old, but it might apply regardless of his age. Much depends upon the state within a country, or the country itself, so check with your veterinarian if the breeder has not already advised you on this.

FEEDING YOUR STANDARD SCHNAUZER

Dog owners today are fortunate in that they live in an age when considerable cash has been invested in the study of canine nutritional requirements. This means dog food manufacturers are very concerned about ensuring that their foods are of the best quality. The result of all of their studies, apart from the food itself, is that dog owners are bombarded

Puppies need a good-quality dog food that promotes the growth and provides them with the energy they require. This little guy pooped out in the middle of dinner. Owner, Kathy Koehler.

with advertisements telling them why they must purchase a given brand. The number of products available to you is unlimited, so it is hardly surprising to find that dogs in general suffer from obesity and an excess of vitamins, rather than the reverse. Be sure to feed age-appropriate food—puppy food up to one year of age, adult food thereafter. Generally breeders recommend dry food supplemented by canned, if needed.

FACTORS AFFECTING NUTRITIONAL NEEDS

Activity Level. A dog that lives in a country environment and is able to exercise for long periods of the day will need more food than the same breed of dog living in an apartment and given little exercise.

Quality of the Food. Obviously the quality of food will affect the quantity required by a puppy. If the nutritional content of a food is low then the puppy will need more of it than if a better quality food was fed.

Balance of Nutrients and Vitamins. Feeding a puppy the correct balance of nutrients is not easy because the average person is not able to measure out ratios of one to another, so it is a case of trying to see that nothing is in excess. However, only tests, or your veterinarian, can be the source of reliable advice.

Genetic and Biological Variation. Apart from all of the other considerations, it should be remembered that each puppy is an individual. His genetic make-up will influence not only his physical characteristics but also his metabolic efficiency. This being so, two pups from the same litter can vary quite a bit in the amount of food they need to perform the same function under the same conditions. If you consider the potential combinations of all of these factors then you will see that pups of a given breed could vary quite a bit in the amount of food they will need. Before discussing feeding quantities it is valuable to know at least a little about the composition of food and its role in the body.

When choosing a diet for your Standard Schnauzer, you should take into consideration his age, lifestyle and energy level. A lounging Schnauzer with owner Barbara Saylor.

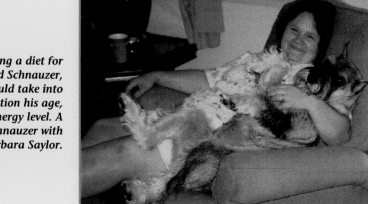

COMPOSITION AND ROLE OF FOOD

The main ingredients of food are protein, fats, and carbohydrates, each of which is needed in relatively large quantities when compared to the other needs of vitamins and minerals. The other vital ingredient of food is, of course, water. Although all foods obviously contain some of the basic ingredients needed for an animal to survive, they do not all contain the ingredients in the needed ratios or type. For example, there are many forms of protein, just as there are many types of carbohydrates. Both of these compounds are found in meat and in vegetable matter—but not all of those that are needed will be in one particular meat or vegetable. Plants, especially, do not contain certain amino acids that are required for the synthesis of certain proteins needed by dogs.

A well-balanced diet will be evident in your Standard Schnauzer's shiny coat and overall healthy appearance.

Likewise, vitamins are found in meats and vegetable matter, but vegetables are a richer source of most. Meat contains very little carbohydrates. Some vitamins can be synthesized by the dog, so do not need to be supplied via the food. Dogs are carnivores and this means their digestive tract has evolved to need a high quantity of meat as compared to humans. The digestive system of carnivores is unable to break down the tough cellulose walls of plant matter, but it is easily able to assimilate proteins from meat.

In order to gain its needed vegetable matter in a form that it can cope with, the carnivore eats all of its prey. This includes the partly digested food

Standard Schnauzers are famous for their love of "people" food; however, it is necessary to provide them with a diet that fits their special canine needs. Owner, Penny Duffee.

within the stomach. In commercially prepared foods, the cellulose is broken down by cooking. During this process the vitamin content is either greatly reduced or lost altogether. The manufacturer therefore adds vitamins once the heat process has been completed. This is why commercial foods are so useful as part of a feeding regimen, providing they are of good quality and from a company that has prepared the foods very carefully.

Proteins

These are made from amino acids, of which at least ten are essential if a puppy is to maintain healthy growth. Proteins provide the building blocks

If you want to change your pup's diet from the one provided by your breeder, do so gradually to avoid stomach upsets.

for the puppy's body. The richest sources are meat, fish and poultry, together with their by-products. The latter will include milk, cheese, yogurt, fishmeal, and eggs. Vegetable matter that has a high protein content includes soy beans, together with numerous corn and other plant extracts that have been dehydrated. The actual protein content needed in the diet will be determined both by the activity level of the dog and his age. The total protein need will also be influenced by the digestibility factor of the food given.

Fats

These serve numerous roles in the puppy's body. They provide insulation against the cold, and help buffer the organs from knocks and general activity shocks. They provide the richest source of energy, and reserves of this, and they are vital in the transport of vitamins and other nutrients, via the blood, to all other organs. Finally, it is the fat content within a diet that gives it palatability. It is important that the fat content of a diet should not be excessive. This is because the high energy content of fats (more than twice that of protein or carbohydrate) will increase the overall energy content of the diet. The puppy will adjust its food intake to that of its energy needs, which are obviously more easily met in a high-energy diet. This will mean that while the fats are providing the energy needs of the puppy, the overall diet may not be providing its protein, vitamin, and mineral needs, so signs of protein deficiency will become apparent. Rich sources of fats are meat, their byproducts (butter, milk), and vegetable oils, such as safflower, olive, corn or soy bean.

Carbohydrates

These are the principal energy compounds given to puppies and adult dogs. Their inclusion within most commercial brand dog foods is for cost, rather than dietary needs. These compounds are more commonly known as sugars, and they are seen in simple or complex compounds of carbon, hydrogen, and oxygen. One of the simple sugars is called glucose, and it is vital to many metabolic processes. When large chains of glucose are created, they form compound sugars. One of these is called glycogen, and it is found in the cells of animals. Another, called starch, is the material that is found in the cells of plants.

It is important that your Standard Schnauzer have plenty of cool clean water available to him at all times.

Vitamins

These are not foods as such but chemical compounds that assist in all aspects of an animal's life. They help in so many ways that to attempt to describe these effectively would require a chapter in itself. Fruits are a rich source of vitamins, as is the liver of most animals. Many vitamins are unstable and easily destroyed by light, heat, moisture, or rancidity. An excess of vitamins, especially A and D, has been proven to be very harmful. Provided a puppy is receiving a balanced diet, it is most unlikely there will be a deficiency, whereas hypervitaminosis (an excess of vitamins) has become quite common due to owners and breeders feeding unneeded supplements. The only time you should feed extra vitamins to your puppy is if your veterinarian advises you to.

Opposite: Your Standard Schnauzer puppy will depend on you, his owner, to provide him with the nutrition he requires.

Minerals

These provide strength to bone and cell tissue, as well as assist in many metabolic processes. Examples are calcium, phosphorous, copper, iron, magnesium, selenium, potassium, zinc, and sodium. The recommended amounts of all minerals in the diet has not been fully established. Calcium and phosphorous are known to be important, especially to puppies. They help in forming strong bone. As with vitamins, a mineral deficiency is most unlikely in pups given a good and varied diet. Again, an excess can create problems—this applying equally to calcium.

Carrots are rich in fiber, carbohydrates, and vitamin A. The Carrot Bone™ by Nylabone® is a durable chew containing no plastics or artificial ingredients and it can be served as-is, in a bone-hard form, or microwaved to a biscuit consistency.

Water

This is the most important of all nutrients, as is easily shown by the fact that the adult dog is made up of about 60 percent water, the puppy containing an even higher percentage. Dogs must retain a water balance, which means that the total intake should be balanced by the total output. The intake comes either by direct input (the tap or its equivalent), plus water released when food is oxidized, known as metabolic water (remember that all foods contain the elements hydrogen and oxygen that recombine in the body to create water). A dog without adequate water will lose condition more rapidly than one depleted of food, a fact common to most animal species.

Opposite: Give your pup a Nylabone® to chew on. It is a tough, durable, completely safe bone that will strengthen your Schnauzer's teeth and jaws.

AMOUNT TO FEED

The best way to determine dietary requirements is by observing the puppy's general health and physical appearance. If he is well covered with flesh, shows good bone development and muscle, and is an active alert puppy, then his diet is fine. A puppy will consume about twice as much as an adult (of the same breed). You should ask the breeder of your puppy to show you the amounts fed to their pups and this will be a good starting point.

The puppy should eat his meal in about five to seven minutes. Any leftover food can be discarded

POPpups™ are 100% edible and enhanced with dog-friendly ingredients like liver, cheese, spinach, chicken, carrots, or potatoes. They contain no salt, sugar, alcohol, plastic or preservatives. You can even microwave a POPpup™ to turn into a huge crackly treat.

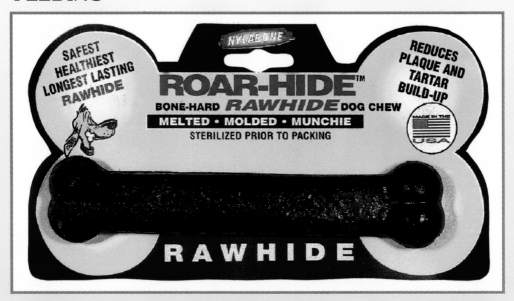

or placed into the refrigerator until the next meal (but be sure it is thawed fully if your fridge is very cold).

If the puppy quickly devours its meal and is clearly still hungry, then you are not giving him enough food. If he eats readily but then begins to pick at it, or walks away leaving a quantity, then you are probably giving him too much food. Adjust this at the next meal and you will quickly begin to appreciate what the correct amount is. If, over a number of weeks, the pup starts to look fat, then he is obviously overeating; the reverse is true if he starts to look thin compared with others of the same breed.

Roar-Hide® is completely edible and is high in protein (over 86%) and low in fat (less than one-third of 1%). Unlike common rawhide, it is safer, less messy, and more fun.

WHEN TO FEED

It really does not matter what times of the day the puppy is fed, as long as he receives the needed quantity of food. Puppies from 8 weeks to 12 or 16 weeks need 3 or 4 meals a day. Older puppies and adult dogs should be fed twice a day. What is most important is that the feeding times are reasonably regular. They can be tailored to fit in with your own timetable—for example, 7 a.m. and 6 p.m. The dog will then expect his meals at these times each day. Keeping regular feeding times and feeding set amounts will help you monitor your puppy's or dog's health. If a dog that's normally enthusiastic about mealtimes and eats readily suddenly shows a lack of interest in food, you'll know something's not right.

TRAINING YOUR STANDARD SCHNAUZER

Standard Schnauzers are highly intelligent dogs that do best when channeling their abilities into events like obedience and agility. AmCan. Ch. Oregonized Julias' Chaz, UD, TDX, AX owned by Robert Kirkbride.

These highly intelligent dogs, if left in charge of their own upbringing, will very quickly take over the day-to-day running of the household. Therefore it is strongly recommended that every Standard Schnauzer should attend obedience classes early in his life. Every Standard deserves an education, and because of the breed's intelligence, every owner of a Standard has to earn an obedient dog. Most breeders and trainers recommend that puppies start formal classes when the pups have had their final immunization shots at approximately 16 weeks of age. Some obedience advocates and breed ring enthusiasts, however, like to take their pups to socialization classes as early as 10 weeks.

By seven weeks of age, the Standard Schnauzer's mind is fully developed and he is ready to be taught the good manners that will make him an accepted part of his family.

The mind of the Standard Schnauzer is fully developed by seven weeks of age and is very similar to a sponge. That sponge can soak up clean water (good manners) or it can learn to soak up dirty water (bad manners). Once learned, bad manners are very difficult to eradicate later in the dog's life.

Schnauzers should be introduced to the dog crate as very young puppies. The crate will be a great asset in housebreaking and preventing chewing problems during the teething stage. Most pups view the crate as their very own private bedroom, and it is a great feeling of security for them to have their "home away from home" when traveling with the family. Never use the crate as a form of punishment. Standards are very bright and intelligent dogs but not bright enough to figure why they are now isolated from the family in the crate. Use the crate at night and during the day when no adult is around to supervise the pup's decision making. Using a wire or plastic crate in a van or wagon is also the safest way to have a dog ride in the family automobile.

Training the Standard can be a lot of fun if the trainer approaches each session with the right attitude. This breed, because of their intelligence, is not quite as forgiving of handler errors as are many other breeds. They are quick learners with a retentive mind. Once they have learned a command, they never forget it. If the Standard Schnauzer is overly bored by repetitive commands, they will often think up some new and ingenious way to do the command. This can sometimes be funny but is often extremely frustrating to the owner who has a background in another breed that requires many repetitions to set a pattern. One important thing to remember with a Standard Schnauzer is that if the dog does it correctly the first time, lavishly praise the dog and go on to something else. Standard Schnauzers do their best work when they are amply rewarded with praise. Owners that have trained their Standard Schnauzer correctly and do competitive obedience or agility work are rewarded with a dog that is fast working and businesslike and

Never situate your Standard Schnauzer's crate too close to a live outlet or another electrical device.

find them placing in the ribbons more often than not. Their very ideal, mid-sized, short-coupled, square structure makes them extremely agile and well suited for all levels of obedience and agility work.

Once your puppy has settled into your home and responds to his name, then you can begin his basic training. Before giving advice on how you should go about doing this, two important points should be made. You should train the puppy in isolation of any potential distractions, and you should keep all lessons very short. It is essential that you have the full

The versatile Standard Schnauzer has the talent and potential to excel in all areas of training. Owners, Dr. Robert and Cathryn Knight.

attention of your puppy. This is not possible if there are other people about, or televisions and radios on, or other pets in the vicinity. Even when the pup has become a young adult, the maximum time you should allocate to a lesson is about 20 minutes. However, you can give the puppy more than one lesson a day, three being as many as are recommended, each well spaced apart.

Before beginning a lesson, always play a little game with the puppy so he is in an active state of mind and thus more receptive to the matter at hand. Likewise, always end a lesson with fun-time for the pup, and always—this is most important—end on a

Training your Standard Schnauzer to wear his collar and leash is one of the easiest tasks you will undertake together.

high note, praising the puppy. Let the lesson end when the pup has done as you require so he receives lots of fuss. This will really build his confidence.

ELIMINATE THE WORD "NO" FROM YOUR DOG'S VOCABULARY

All dogs and especially Standard Schnauzers respond very poorly to negative commands. By eliminating the negative command words and replacing them with positive command words, the pup will learn proper household manners much more quickly and willingly. Most people say the word "No" to their puppy on an average of 20 or 30 or more times a day. Yet most times when they say this word they mean for the dog to stop doing something different. This nagging repetitious use of the word "No" can be very confusing for the young pup. Most intelligent dogs will very quickly learn to tune you out. Let me give you some ideas

For his safety, it is important that your dog become used to walking on lead.

and hints on how you can get your message across to the puppy in a positive way and enable you to eliminate undesirable behavior at the same time.

The "Off" Command

Use this command any time you want the puppy to put his feet back on the ground. For example; "Off" the furniture, "Off" the counter top, "Off" you or "Off" the neighbor. (Do not use the word "Down" because you have already taught the pup that the word "Down" means to place his belly on the floor.)

The "Leave it" or "Mine" Command

Use one of these two commands any time you do not want the dog to sniff, touch or grab an object with his nose or mouth.

The "Drop it" or "Give" Command

Use either of these two commands whenever you want the dog to release what is in his mouth.

It is critical to the teaching of these command words that you lavishly praise the puppy at the very instant that the pup obeys, even if you have to "make" the puppy obey your command. The most important idea to remember when giving any command to your puppy is this: It is not so much *what* you say, as it is *how* you say it. Proper tone of voice is crucial for correct compliance to your command by your pup.

COLLAR AND LEASH TRAINING

Training a puppy to his collar and leash is very easy. Place a "buckle" collar on the puppy and, although he will initially try to bite at it, he will soon forget it, the more so if you play with him. You can leave the collar on for a few hours. Some people leave their dogs' collars on all of the time, others only when they are taking the dog out. If it is to be left on, purchase a narrow or round one so it does not break the coarse guardhairs.

These puppies have mastered the sit command and look like they are awaiting their next lesson! Owner, Kathy Koehler.

Once the puppy ignores his collar, then you can attach the leash to it and let the puppy pull this along behind it for a few minutes. However, if the pup starts to chew at the leash, simply hold the leash but keep it slack and let the pup go where he wants. The idea is to let him get the feel of the leash, but not get in the habit of chewing it. Repeat this a couple of times a day for two days and the pup will get used to the leash without thinking that it will restrain him—which you will not have attempted to do yet.

Next, you can let the pup understand that the leash will restrict his movements. The first time he realizes this, he will pull and buck or just sit down. Immediately call the pup to you and give him lots of fuss. Never tug on the leash so the puppy is dragged along the floor, as this simply implants a negative thought in his mind.

THE COME COMMAND

Teaching the Standard Schnauzer the command "Come" properly is critical to this very bright and independent thinking breed. Never use this command when you are even thinking about punishing your pup. This is one command that you must look at from the dog's point of view. For example, no one in your family was supervising you and no one saw you chewing on the corner of the kitchen cabinet. Two hours later someone yells "Come" and starts to scream at you for something you enjoyed doing that made your hurting gums feel better. It does not take a dog with even average

The epitome of this remarkable breed, Ch. Otch. Tailgate's George Vonpickel, UDX or "George" takes one last lap around the police dog training course before retiring.

intelligence very long to associate the word "Come" with isolation or punishment if you are not careful.

To start teaching the "Come" command properly, it is best accomplished if you get down to the dog's level on the floor. Make some funny noises, or use a squeaky toy, to first get the pup's attention. Promptly say the puppy's name and "Come" in a very pleasant and exciting tone of voice. As the pup is moving toward you, repeat the words "good, good, good" several times in a very pleasant and exciting tone of voice to help hasten his journey toward you. When the

This Standard Schnauzer shows his exceptional scenting abilities in the scent discrimination exercise in the Utility Class. Owner, Barbara Dille.

pup gets to you, lavishly praise him for 10 to 15 seconds while repeating the word "Come." Initially, you can add a small food treat, or a favorite toy, as an extra incentive in addition to your lavish verbal praise as a reward for obeying this command. Let the pup go for 30 seconds or so and repeat this two more times. This three-time sequence should be repeated several times each day at least once a week. You can also use this word just as you are giving the pup his meals, water, or a favorite toy.

Remember, while in the puppy stage, the word "Come" should *always* mean pleasure to the dog. If

The Standard Schnauzer as a breed does not have an instinctual love of water, but there are exceptions—especially when it's hot.

you want to call the dog to you to put him in his crate or to come inside the house, the important thing to remember is that you must give the pup that initial 10- to 15-second period of lavish praise for obeying the "Come" command first, then you can give the dog the next command of "In the house" or "Crate time."

THE SIT COMMAND

As with most basic commands, your puppy will learn this one in just a few lessons. Some trainers will advise you that you should not proceed to other commands until the previous one has been learned really well. However, a bright young pup is quite capable of handling more than one command per lesson, and certainly per day. This is so the puppy always starts, as well as ends, a training session on a high note, having successfully completed something.

Call the puppy to you and fuss over him. Place one hand on his hindquarters and the other under his upper chest. Say "Sit" in a pleasant (never harsh) voice. At the same time, push down his rear end and place your hand under the pup's lower jaw and tilt the pup's head up so he is looking at you with direct eye contact. Now lavish praise on the puppy. Repeat this a few times and your pet will get the idea. Once the puppy is in the sit position you will release your hands. At first he will tend to get up, so immediately repeat the exercise. Do not attempt to keep the pup in the sit position for too long. At this age, even a few seconds is a long while and you do not want him to get bored with lessons before he has even begun them.

THE DOWN COMMAND

From the viewpoint of the Standard Schnauzer, the "Down" command can be one of the more difficult ones to accept. The down position is normally taken only when the puppy is tired or acting submissive. There are several methods to obtain the goal of the down position. I have found the following one to be the most successful with the independent-minded young Standard Schnauzer puppy. Start by taking an irresistible small piece of food in your right hand. Place your hand holding the food directly next to the pup's nose. Slowly move your hand with the food down to the floor to a position right between the dog's front paws. Your hand must move slowly as if the food was a magnet

Uhlan Legend, CDX, owned by Dr. Robert and Cathryn Knight, shown negotiating the dog walk at an agility trial.

and the dog's nose was attached to the magnet. While putting some pressure with your left hand on the pup's shoulder, slowly and firmly say the word "Down." Draw the word out so it comes out "Do-o-o-o-own." Immediately, once the pup has his belly on the floor, give him the food and scratch his shoulder area while lavishly praising him with: "Good boy—down."

THE STAND COMMAND

The "Stand" is a must-do command not only for the show dog but for any breed like the Standard Schnauzer that requires extensive grooming while he is in the standing position. Start with the dog in the sit position. Place your right hand in the pup's buckle collar underneath his chin. Verbally say "Sta-a-a-a-and" while pulling gently forward with your right hand. Meanwhile scratch your pup's tummy with your left hand while *gently* lifting his rear end into a standing position. Briefly and lightly hold the dog in this stand position and praise lavishly.

THE STAY COMMAND

This command is used after the pup has assumed any one of the positions of sit, stand or down. It is

Demonstrating the tractability of the Standard Schnauzer, George worked in various neighborhoods teaching responsible pet ownership and promoting canine good citizenship.

A well-trained Standard Schnauzer is a pleasure and will be welcomed in any home. Ch. Artaxerxes Von Molloy, UD and Ch. Morgenwald's Darya Anastasia, UD, owned by Dr. Robert and Cathryn Knight.

most easily taught first when following the command "Sit." With the pup on a leash in a sit position on your left side, give the pup the verbal command "Sta-a-a-ay." Simultaneously move your right hand abruptly to a quick stop position ending approximately one inch in front of the pup's nose. Make this a definite command word with a firm (but not loud) tone of "do it," not in a pleading tone of "ple-e-ease do it."

Hesitate approximately one or two seconds and move slowly away from the pup approximately three feet. Turn and face the pup. Count to five and then return to the pup's side. Release the puppy from the stay position with a command of "good boy, all done." If the pup moves before your release command, gently place him back in the start position, and go from the beginning of the command again. Very gradually over a period of weeks, increase the length of time the pup is required to stay and lengthen the distance you go from him. Practice this command on the sit, the down and stand positions at least once a day.

AmCan. Ch. Oregonized Julia's Chaz, UD, TDX, AX shows the dexterity and quickness of the Standard Schnauzer by mastering the weave pole obstacle. Owner, Robert Kirkbride.

LOOSE LEAD WALKING

All dogs should be able to walk quietly on a leash and not involve their owners in a tug-of-war. Introduce the puppy to a buckle collar. Once the puppy is used to the collar, attach a narrow, very lightweight leash to the collar. Allow the pup to drag the leash around for a few minutes. When the pup seems comfortable with this, go to the next step.

Pick up the end of the leash and pat your leg, using the command "Let's go." Start to move slowly away from the pup while encouraging with lavish praise for the dog to follow you. If the pup starts to run ahead of you, quickly stop. While giving a very gentle but quick tug on the leash, turn 180 degrees from the direction the pup is headed and take a few steps in the new direction, continuing with your lavish praise. Continue this walking and changing direction for no more than one or two minutes. Take the leash off the puppy and play with him for a few minutes with one of his favorite toys. For the next 15 or 20 minutes, repeat this process no more than three times. Within just a few

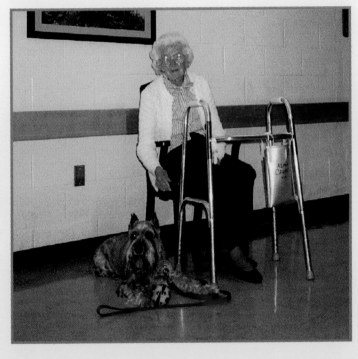

The time you spend training your Standard Schnauzer will allow you and your dog to form a close bond. Therapy dog Alfie and a special friend. Owner, Cindy Crumb.

days your puppy should be walking very nicely on a loose leash with the command "Let's go."

THE HEEL COMMAND

This command is taught after the puppy is no longer playing tug-of-war with you when on a leash. One can find many different ways to teach this command. The objective is to have your dog focus all attention on you. The dog must ignore everything else in the environment when he is on this command. The dog is not supposed to stop and eliminate or even sniff a tree or the grass. Because the young Standard Schnauzer puppy has a very inquisitive and active mind, I suggest that this command not be attempted on the very young puppy at all. Wait until the puppy is five to six months old before starting this demanding command. When you do start teaching this command, alternate between loose lead walking and heeling, with the heeling lesson lasting no more than 30 seconds at a time. Starting with the dog in a sit position on your left side, step off with your left foot first while saying the dog's name and the command "Heel." At first, do anything you want with your hands, voice or even a toy that enables you to keep your dog's total attention on you. For perfect heel position while walking, the dog's neck should be opposite the midline of your hip and the dog should be no more than six inches away from your leg. When you stop, repeat the word "Heel" while helping the dog into a sitting position by your left heel. When the dog is keeping this very precise heel position for a few yards in a straight line, it is time to add some about-turns, small circles to the left and to the right. During these maneuvers, make sure that the dog does not stray from the desired position. When finished with this command, release the dog from the command with an "Okay—all done" or some other phrase.

Opposite: With the proper training, who knows how far your Standard Schnauzer can go! Ch. Ahrenfelds Iron Wolf V. Vortas bred by Shelly Wiggins and Barbara Dille.

A Standard Schnauzer returning over the solid jump in the utility ring.

YOUR HEALTHY STANDARD SCHNAUZER

Dogs, like all other animals, are capable of contracting problems and diseases that, in most cases, are easily avoided by sound husbandry—meaning well-bred and well-cared-for animals are less prone to developing diseases and problems than are carelessly bred and neglected animals. Your knowledge of how to avoid problems is far more valuable than all of the books and advice on how to cure them. Respectively, the only person you should listen to about treatment is your vet. Veterinarians don't have all the answers, but at least they are trained to analyze and treat illnesses, and are aware of the full implications of treatments. This does not mean a few old remedies aren't good standbys when all else fails, but in most cases modern science provides the best treatments for disease.

Opposite: Author Barbara M. Dille has been raising and training dogs since the 1950s. Her Vortac prefix of Standard Schnauzers was established in the 1960s. Here she is pictured with one of her dogs, Ch. Vortac Autumn Legacy, CGC.

PHYSICAL EXAMS

Your puppy should receive regular physical examinations or check-ups. These come in two forms. One is obviously performed by your vet, and the other is a day-to-day procedure that should be done by you. Apart from the fact the exam will highlight any problem at an early stage, it is an excellent way of socializing the pup to being handled.

To do the physical exam yourself, start at the head and work your way around the body. You are looking for any sign of lesions, or any indication of parasites on the pup. The most common parasites are fleas and ticks.

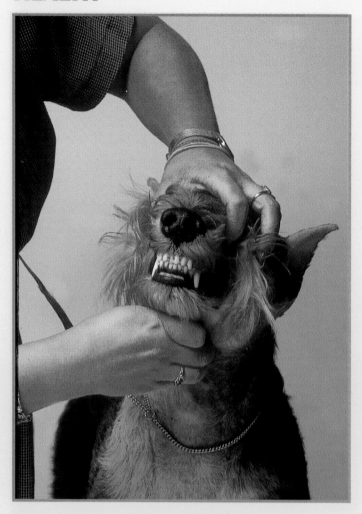

A thorough oral exam should be a part of of your Standard Schnauzer's regular veterinary check-up.

HEALTHY TEETH AND GUMS

Chewing is instinctual. Puppies chew so that their teeth and jaws grow strong and healthy as they develop. As the permanent teeth begin to emerge, it is painful and annoying to the puppy, and puppy owners must recognize that their new charges need something safe upon which to chew. Unfortunately, once the puppy's permanent teeth have emerged and settled solidly into the jaw, the chewing instinct does not fade. Adult dogs instinctively need to clean their teeth, massage their gums, and exercise their jaws through chewing.

It is necessary for your dog to have clean teeth. You should take your dog to the veterinarian at least once a year to have his teeth cleaned and to have his mouth examined for any sign of oral disease. Although dogs do not get cavities in the same way humans do, dogs'

The Hercules™ by Nylabone® has raised dental tips that help fight plaque on your Standard Schnauzer's teeth and gums.

teeth accumulate tartar, and more quickly than humans do! Veterinarians recommend brushing your dog's teeth daily. But who can find time to brush their dog's teeth daily? The accumulation of tartar and plaque on our dog's teeth when not removed can cause irritation and eventually erode the enamel and finally destroy the teeth. Advanced cases, while destroying the teeth, bring on gingivitis and periodontitis, two very serious conditions that can affect the dog's internal organs as well...to say nothing about bad breath!

Since everyone can't brush their dog's teeth daily or get to the veterinarian often enough for him to scale

Nylafloss® does wonders for your Standard Schnauzer's dental health by massaging his gums and literally flossing between his teeth, loosening plaque and tartar build-up. Unlike cotton tug toys, Nylafloss® won't rot or fray.

the dog's teeth, providing the dog with something safe to chew on will help maintain oral hygeine. Chew devices from Nylabone® keep dogs' teeth clean, but they also provide an excellent resource for entertainment and relief of doggie tensions. Nylabone® products give your dog something to do for an hour or two every day and during that hour or two, your dog will be taking an active part in keeping his teeth and gums healthy...without even realizing it! That's invaluable to your dog, and valuable to you!

Nylabone® provides fun bones, challenging bones, and *safe* bones. It is an owner's responsibility to recognize safe chew toys from dangerous ones. Your dog will chew and devour anything you give him. Dogs must not be permitted to chew on items that they can break. Pieces of broken objects can do internal damage to a dog, besides ripping the dog's mouth. Cheap plastic or rubber toys can cause stoppage in the intestines; such stoppages are operable only if caught immediately.

The most obvious choices, in this case, may be the worst choice. Natural beef bones were not designed for chewing and cannot take too much pressure from the sides. Due to the abrasive nature of these bones, they should be offered most sparingly. Knuckle bones, though once very popular for dogs, can be easily

Nylabone® is the only plastic dog bone made of 100% virgin nylon, specially processed to create a tough, durable, completely safe bone.

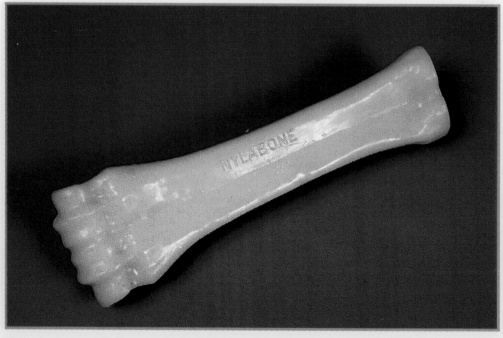

Chick-n-Cheez Chooz® are completely safe and nutritious health chews made from pure cheese protein, chicken, and fortified with vitamin E. They contain no salt, sugar, plastic, or preservatives and less than 1% fat.

chewed up and eaten by dogs. At the very least, digestion is interrupted; at worst, the dog can choke or suffer from intestinal blockage.

When a dog chews hard on a Nylabone®, little bristle-like projections appear on the surface of the bone. These help to clean the dog's teeth and add to the gum-massaging. Given the chemistry of the nylon, the bristle can pass through the dog's intestinal tract without effect. Since nylon is inert, no microorganism can grow on it, and it can be washed in soap and water or sterilized in boiling water or in an autoclave.

For the sake of your dog, his teeth and your own peace of mind, provide your dog with Nylabones®. They have 100 variations from which to choose.

FIGHTING FLEAS

Fleas are very mobile and may be red, black, or brown in color. The adults suck the blood of the host, while the larvae feed on the feces of the adults, which is rich in blood. Flea "dirt" may be seen on the pup as very tiny clusters of blackish specks that look like freshly ground pepper. The eggs of fleas may be laid on the puppy, though they are more commonly laid off the host in a favorable place, such as the bedding. They normally hatch in 4 to 21 days, depending on the temperature, but they can survive for up to 18 months if temperature conditions are not favorable. The larvae are maggot-like and molt a couple of times before forming pupae, which can survive long periods until the temperature, or the vibration of a nearby host, causes them to emerge and jump on a host.

There are a number of effective treatments available, and you should discuss them with your veterinarian, then follow all instructions for the one you choose. Any treatment will involve a product for your puppy or dog and one for the environment, and will require diligence on your part to treat all areas and thoroughly clean your home and yard until the infestation is eradicated.

THE TROUBLE WITH TICKS

Ticks are arthropods of the spider family, which means they have eight legs (though the larvae have six). They bury their headparts into the host and gorge on its blood. They are easily seen as small grain-like creatures sticking out from the skin. They are often picked up when dogs play in fields, but may also arrive in your yard via wild animals—even birds—or stray cats and dogs. Some ticks are species-specific, others are more adaptable and will host on many species.

The cat flea is the most common flea of dogs. It starts feeding soon after it makes contact with the dog.

The deer tick is the most common carrier of Lyme disease. Photo courtesy of Virbac Laboratories, Inc., Fort Worth, Texas.

The most troublesome type of tick is the deer tick, which spreads the deadly Lyme disease that can cripple a dog (or a person). Deer ticks are tiny and very hard to detect. Often, by the time they're big enough to notice, they've been feeding on the dog for a few days—long enough to do their damage. Lyme disease was named for the area of the United States in which it was first detected—Lyme, Connecticut—but has now been diagnosed in almost all parts of the U.S. Your veterinarian can advise you of the danger to your dog(s) in your area, and may suggest your dog be vaccinated for Lyme. Always go over your dog with a fine-toothed flea comb when you come in from walking through any area that may harbor deer ticks, and if your dog is acting unusually sluggish or sore, seek veterinary advice.

Attempts to pull a tick free will invariably leave the headpart in the pup, where it will die and cause an infected wound or abscess. The best way to remove ticks is to dab a strong saline solution, iodine, or alcohol on them. This will numb them, causing them to loosen their hold, at which time they can be removed with forceps. The wound can then be cleaned and covered with an antiseptic ointment. If ticks are common in your area, consult with your vet for a suitable pesticide to be used in kennels, on bedding, and on the puppy or dog.

INSECTS AND OTHER OUTDOOR DANGERS

There are many biting insects, such as mosquitoes, that can cause discomfort to a puppy. Many diseases are transmitted by the males of these species.

A pup can easily get a grass seed or thorn lodged between his pads or in the folds of his ears. These may go unnoticed until an abscess forms.

This is where your daily check of the puppy or dog will do a world of good. If your puppy has been playing in long grass or places where there may be thorns, pine needles, wild animals, or parasites, the check-up is a wise precaution.

SKIN DISORDERS

Apart from problems associated with lesions created by biting pests, a puppy may fall foul to a number of other skin disorders. Examples are ringworm, mange, and eczema. Ringworm is not caused by a worm, but is a fungal infection. It manifests itself as a sore-looking bald circle. If your puppy should have any form of bald patches, let your veterinarian check him over; a microscopic examination can confirm the condition. Many old remedies for ringworm exist, such as iodine, carbolic acid, formalin, and other tinctures, but modern drugs are superior.

Make sure you check your Standard Schnauzer's coat thoroughly for parasites like fleas and ticks after he has been outside.

Fungal infections can be very difficult to treat, and even more difficult to eradicate, because of the spores. These can withstand most treatments, other than burning, which is the best thing to do with bedding once the condition has been confirmed.

Mange is a general term that can be applied to many skin conditions where the hair falls out and a flaky crust develops and falls away.

Often, dogs will scratch themselves, and this invariably is worse than the original condition, for it opens lesions that are then subject to viral, fungal, or parasitic attack. The cause of the problem can be various species of mites. These either live on skin debris and the hair follicles, which they destroy, or they bury themselves just beneath the skin and feed on the tissue. Applying general remedies from pet stores is not recommended because it is essential to identify the type of mange before a specific treatment is effective.

Eczema is another non-specific term applied to many skin disorders. The condition can be brought about in many ways. Sunburn, chemicals, allergies to foods, drugs, pollens, and even stress can all produce a deterioration of the skin and coat. Given the range of causal factors, treatment can be difficult because the problem is one of identification. It is a case of taking each possibility at a time and trying to correctly diagnose the matter. If the cause is of a dietary nature then you must remove one item at a time in order to find out if the dog is allergic to a given food. It could, of course, be the lack of a nutrient that is the problem, so if the condition persists, you should consult your veterinarian.

INTERNAL DISORDERS

It cannot be overstressed that it is very foolish to attempt to diagnose an internal disorder without the advice of a veterinarian. Take a relatively common problem such as diarrhea. It might be caused by nothing more serious than the puppy hogging a lot of food or eating something that it has never previously eaten. Conversely, it could be the first indication of a potentially fatal disease. It's up to your veterinarian to make the correct diagnosis.

The following symptoms, especially if they accompany each other or are progressively added to earlier symptoms, mean you should visit the veterinarian right away:

Continual vomiting. All dogs vomit from time to time and this is not necessarily a sign of illness. They will eat grass to induce vomiting. It is a natural cleansing process common to many carnivores. However, continued vomiting is a clear sign of a problem. It may be a blockage in the pup's intestinal tract, it may be induced by worms, or it could be due to any number of diseases.

Diarrhea. This, too, may be nothing more than a temporary condition due to many factors. Even a change of home can induce diarrhea, because this often stresses the pup, and invariably there is some change in the diet. If it persists more than 48 hours then something is amiss. If blood is seen in the feces, waste no time at all in taking the dog to the vet.

Running eyes and/or nose. A pup might have a chill and this will cause the eyes and nose to weep. Again, this should quickly clear up if the puppy is placed in a warm environment and away from any drafts. If it does not, and especially if a mucous discharge is seen, then the pup has an illness that must be diagnosed.

Coughing. Prolonged coughing is a sign of a problem, usually of a respiratory nature.

Wheezing. If the pup has difficulty breathing and makes a wheezing sound when breathing, then something is wrong.

Cries when attempting to defecate or urinate. This might only be a minor problem due to the hard state of the feces, but it could be more serious, especially if the pup cries when urinating.

Cries when touched. Obviously, if you do not handle a puppy with care he might yelp. However, if he cries even when lifted gently, then he has an internal problem that becomes apparent when pressure is applied to a given area of the body. Clearly, this must be diagnosed.

Refuses food. Generally, puppies and dogs are greedy creatures when it comes to feeding time. Some might be more fussy, but none should refuse more than one meal. If they go for a number of hours without showing any interest in their food, then something is not as it should be.

General listlessness. All puppies have their off days when they do not seem their usual cheeky, mischievous selves. If this condition persists for more than two days then there is little doubt of a problem. They may not show any of the signs listed, other than perhaps a reduced interest in their food. There are many diseases that can develop internally without displaying obvious clinical signs. Blood, fecal, and other tests are needed in order to identify the disorder before it reaches an advanced state that may not be treatable.

WORMS

There are many species of worms, and a number of these live in the tissues of dogs and most other animals. Many create no problem at all, so you are not even aware they exist. Others can be tolerated in small levels, but become a major problem if they number more than a few. The most common types seen in dogs are roundworms and tapeworms. While roundworms are the greater problem, tapeworms require an intermediate host so are more easily eradicated.

Roundworms of the species *Toxocara canis* infest the dog. They may grow to a length of 8 inches (20 cm) and

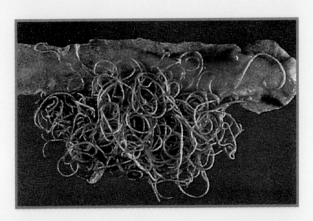

Roundworms are spaghetti-like worms that cause a pot-bellied appearance and dull coat, along with more severe symptoms, such as diarrhea and vomiting. Photo courtesy of Merck AgVet.

look like strings of spaghetti. The worms feed on the digesting food in the pup's intestines. In chronic cases the puppy will become pot-bellied, have diarrhea, and will vomit. Eventually, he will stop eating, having passed through the stage when he always seems hungry. The worms lay eggs in the puppy and these pass out in his feces. They are then either ingested by the pup, or they are eaten by mice, rats, or beetles. These may then be eaten by the puppy and the life cycle is complete.

Larval worms can migrate to the womb of a pregnant bitch, or to her mammary glands, and this is how they pass to the puppy. Prior to being bred, the bitch should be wormed to prevent infestation of pups. The pups can, and should, be wormed when they are about five or six weeks old. Repeat worming every 10 to 14 days and the parasites should be removed. Worms can be

Whipworms are hard to find unless you strain your dog's feces, and this is best left to a veterinarian. Pictured here are adult whipworms.

extremely dangerous to young puppies, so you should be sure the pup is wormed as a matter of routine.

Tapeworms can be seen as tiny rice-like eggs sticking to the puppy's or dog's anus. They are less destructive, but still undesirable. The eggs are eaten by mice, fleas, rabbits, and other animals that serve as intermediate hosts. They develop into a larval stage and the host or its feces must be eaten by the dog in order to complete the chain. Ingesting infected fleas is the most common way for dogs to acquire tapeworms. Your vet will supply a suitable remedy if tapeworms are seen or suspected. There are other worms, such as hookworms and whipworms, that are also blood suckers. They will make a pup anemic, and blood might be seen in the feces, which can be examined by the vet to confirm their presence. Cleanliness in all matters is the best preventative measure for all worms.

Heartworm infestation in dogs is passed by mosquitoes but can be prevented by a monthly (or daily) treatment that is given orally. Talk to your vet about the risk of heartworm in your area.

BLOAT (GASTRIC DILATATION)

This condition has proved fatal in many dogs, especially large and deep-chested breeds, such as the Weimaraner and the Great Dane. However, any dog can get bloat. It is caused by swallowing air during exercise, food/water gulping or another strenuous task. As many believe, it is not the result of flatulence. The stomach of an affected dog twists, disallowing food and blood flow and resulting in harmful toxins being released into the bloodstream. Death can easily follow if the condition goes undetected.

The best preventative measure is not to feed large meals or exercise your puppy or dog immediately after he has eaten. Veterinarians recommend feeding three smaller meals per day in an elevated feeding rack, adding water to dry food to prevent gulping, and not offering water during mealtimes.

VACCINATIONS

Every puppy, purebred or mixed breed, should be vaccinated against the major canine diseases. These are distemper, leptospirosis, hepatitis, and canine parvovirus. Your puppy may have received a temporary vaccination against distemper before you purchased him, but be sure to ask the breeder to be sure.

The age at which vaccinations are given can vary, but will usually be when the pup is 5 to 6 weeks old. By this time any protection given to the pup by antibodies received from his mother via her initial milk feeds will be losing their strength.

Rely on your veterinarian for the most effectual vaccination schedule for your Standard Schnauzer puppy.

The puppy's immune system works on the basis that the white blood cells engulf and render harmless

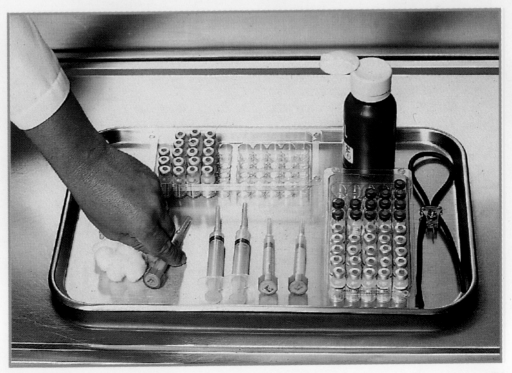

attacking bacteria. However, they must first recognize a potential enemy.

Vaccines are either dead bacteria or they are live, but in very small doses. Either type prompts the pup's defense system to attack them. When a large attack then comes (if it does), the immune system recognizes it and massive numbers of lymphocytes (white blood corpuscles) are mobilized to counter the attack. However, the ability of the cells to recognize these dangerous viruses can diminish over a period of time. It is therefore useful to provide annual reminders about the nature of the enemy. This is done by means of booster injections that keep the immune system on its alert. Immunization is not 100-percent guaranteed to be successful, but is very close. Certainly it is better than giving the puppy no protection.

Dogs are subject to other viral attacks, and if these are of a high-risk factor in your area, then your vet will suggest you have the puppy vaccinated against these as well.

Your puppy or dog should also be vaccinated against the deadly rabies virus. In fact, in many places it is illegal for your dog not to be vaccinated. This is to protect your dog, your family, and the rest of the animal population from this deadly virus that infects the nervous system and causes dementia and death.

ACCIDENTS

All puppies will get their share of bumps and bruises due to the rather energetic way they play. These will usually heal themselves over a few days. Small cuts should be bathed with a suitable disinfectant and then smeared with an antiseptic ointment. If a cut looks more serious, then stem the flow of blood with a towel or makeshift tourniquet and rush the pup to the veterinarian. Never apply so much pressure to the wound that it might restrict the flow of blood to the limb.

In the case of burns you should apply cold water or an ice pack to the surface. If the burn was due to a chemical, then this must be washed away with copious amounts of water. Apply petroleum jelly, or any vegetable oil, to the burn. Trim away the hair if need be. Wrap the dog in a blanket and rush him to the vet. The pup may go into shock, depending on the severity of the burn, and this will result in a lowered blood pressure, which is dangerous and the reason the pup must receive immediate veterinary attention.

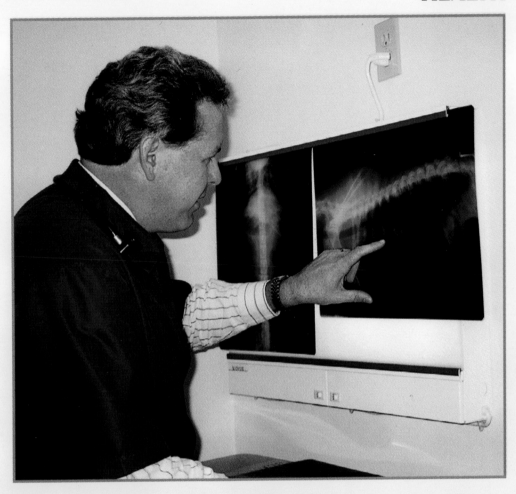

It is a good idea to x-ray the chest and abdomen on any dog hit by a car.

If a broken limb is suspected then try to keep the animal as still as possible. Wrap your pup or dog in a blanket to restrict movement and get him to the veterinarian as soon as possible. Do not move the dog's head so it is tilting backward, as this might result in blood entering the lungs.

Do not let your pup jump up and down from heights, as this can cause considerable shock to the joints. Like all youngsters, puppies do not know when enough is enough, so you must do all their thinking for them.

Provided you apply strict hygiene to all aspects of raising your puppy, and you make daily checks on his physical state, you have done as much as you can to safeguard him during his most vulnerable period. Routine visits to your veterinarian are also recommended, especially while the puppy is under one year of age. The vet may notice something that did not seem important to you.

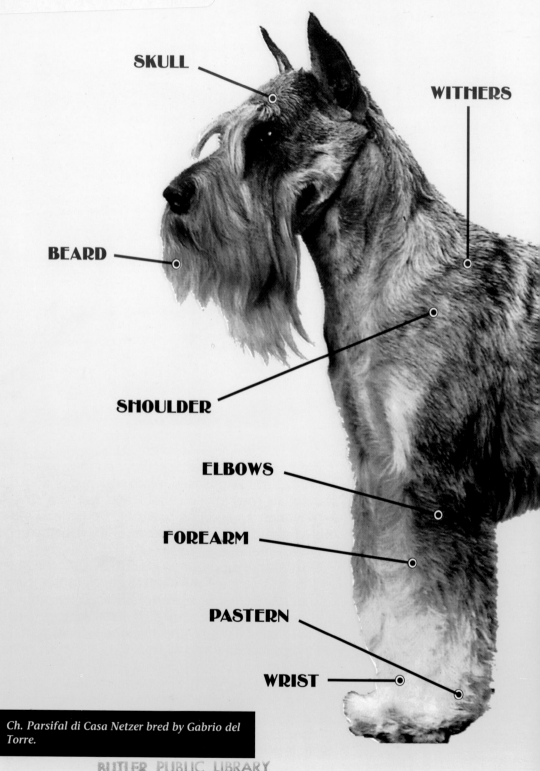

SKULL

WITHERS

BEARD

SHOULDER

ELBOWS

FOREARM

PASTERN

WRIST

Ch. Parsifal di Casa Netzer bred by Gabrio del Torre.